Supplicatory Canon and Akathist
to
Saint Herman of Alaska

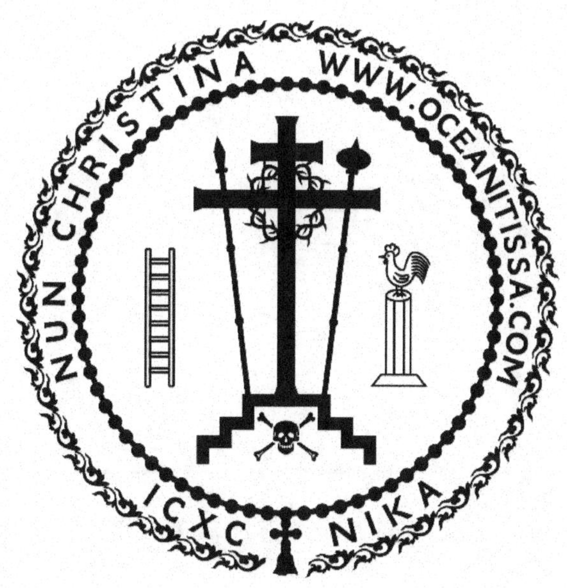

Nun Christina
Anna Skoubourdis

Published by: Virgin Mary of Australia and Oceania 2022 ©
oceanitissa@gmail.com
www.oceanitissa.com.au
Youtube: Nun Christina Oceanitissa

Troparia and Kontakia

Troparion — Grave Tone (7th)
O joyful north star of the Church of Christ, / guiding all men to the Heavenly
Kingdom; / teacher and apostle of the true faith; / intercessor and defender of the
oppressed. / Adornment of the Orthodox Church in America, / blessed Father
Herman of Alaska, / pray to our Lord Jesus Christ / for the salvation of our souls!

Troparion — Tone 4
O blessed Father Herman of Alaska, / north star of Christ's holy Church, / the light
of your holy life and great deeds / guides those who follow the Orthodox way. /
Together we lift high the Holy Cross / you planted firmly in America. / Let all
behold and glorify Jesus Christ, / singing his holy Resurrection.

Kontakion — Tone 3
The eternal light of Christ our Savior, / guided you, O blessed father Herman, / on
your evangelical journey to America, / proclaiming the Gospel of peace. / Now you
stand before the throne of Glory; / intercede for your land and its people / peace for
the world and salvation for our souls!

St. Herman, Wonderworker of Alaska, Troparion, Tone 4
O venerable Herman, ascetic of the northern wilderness/ and gracious advocate for
all the world,/ teacher of the Orthodox Faith and good, instructor of piety,/
adornment of Alaska and joy of all America;// Entreat Christ God, that He save our
souls.

Kontakion for St. Herman, Tone Plagal 4th (8)
O beloved of the Mother of God, who received the tonsure at Valaam,/ new zealot
of the struggles of the desert-dwellers of old:/ wielding prayer as a spear and shield,
thou didst show thyself to be terrible to demons and pagan darkness.// Wherefore,
we cry out to thee: O venerable Herman, entreat Christ God, that our souls be
saved!

Supplicatory Canon

Priest: Blessed is our God always, now and forever and to the ages of ages.
People: Amen.

Psalm 142
O Lord, hear my prayer, give ear to my supplications in Your truth; hear me in Your righteousness. Do not enter into judgment, with Your servant, for in Your sight no one living is justified. For the enemy has persecuted my soul; he has crushed my life to the ground; he has made me dwell in darkness, like those who have long been dead, and my spirit is overwhelmed within me; my heart within me is distressed. I remembered the days of old; I meditated on all Your works: I pondered on the work of Your hands. I spread out my hands to You; my soul longs for You, like a thirsty land. Hear me quickly, O Lord; my spirit fails. Do not turn Your face away from me, lest I be like those who go down into the pit. Cause me to hear Your mercy in the morning, for in You I have put my trust. Cause me to know, O Lord, the way in which I should walk, for I lift up my soul to You. Rescue me, lord, from my enemies; to You have I fled for refuge. Teach me to do Your will, for You are my God. Your good Spirit shall lead me in the land of uprightness. For Your name's sake, O Lord, You shall quicken me. In Your righteousness You shall bring my soul out of trouble, and in Your mercy, You shall utterly destroy my enemies. And you shall destroy all those who afflict my soul; for I am Your servant.

Tone 4

God is the Lord; and has revealed Himself to us, blessed is he who comes in the name of the Lord.

Give thanks to the Lord and call upon His holy name.

.
God is the Lord; and has revealed Himself to us, blessed is he who comes in the name of the Lord.

All the nations have surrounded me, but in the name of the Lord, I have overcome them.

God is the Lord and has revealed Himself to us; blessed is he who comes in the name of the Lord.

This has been done by the Lord, and it is wonderful in our eyes.

God is the Lord and has revealed Himself to us; blessed is he who comes in the name of the Lord.

Tone 4 "He who was raised up"
You, the Pure Equal-of the Apostles of Alaska, because of your heart of love and prayer toward all the inhabited earth, with longing from the depths of our hearts, we

the ranks of the pious, praise you, O righteous Herman, with sacred songs; let us also ask your fervent prayers before the Lord!

Glory to the Father and the Son and the Holy Spirit.

(Repeat the above or the Apolytikion of the Church)

Now and forever and to the ages of ages. Amen.

O Theotokos, we shall never be silent of your mighty acts, all we the unworthy; had you not stood to intercede for us who would have delivered us, from the numerous perils? Who would have preserved us all until now with our freedom? O Lady, we shall not depart from you; for you always save your servants, from all tribulation.

Psalm 50
Have mercy on me, O God, according to Your great mercy; and according to the multitude of Your compassion blot out my transgression. Wash me thoroughly from my iniquity, and cleanse me from my sin. For I acknowledge my iniquity, and my sin is ever before me. Against You, You only, have I sinned, and done this evil in Your sight, that You may be found just when You speak, and blameless when You judge. For behold, I was conceived in iniquity, and in sin my mother bore me. For behold, You have loved truth: You have made known to me the secret things of Your wisdom. You shall sprinkle me with hyssop, and I shall be made clean: You shall wash me, and I shall be whiter than snow. Make me to hear joy and gladness, that bones which You have broken may rejoice. Turn Your face away from my sins, and blot out all my iniquities. Create in me a clean heart, O God, and renew a steadfast spirit within me. Do not cast me away from Your presence, and do not take Your Holy Spirit from me. Restore to me the joy of Your salvation: And establish me with Your governing Spirit. I shall teach transgressors Your ways, and the ungodly shall turn back to You. Deliver me from bloodguiltiness, O God, the God of my salvation, my tongue shall rejoice in Your righteousness. O Lord, open my lips, and my mouth shall show forth Your praise. For if You had desired sacrifice, I would give it: You do not delight in burnt offering. A sacrifice to God is a broken spirit, God will not despise a broken and humbled heart. Do good in Your good pleasure to Sion; and let the walls of Jerusalem be built. Then You shall be pleased with a sacrifice of righteousness., with oblation and whole burnt offerings. Then they shall offer calves on Your altar.

The Canon in Plagal 4th (8th) Tone,

Ode 1 "Crossing the Waters..."

O Father Herman, the divinely dawning, you shone forth with prudence in asceticism and offering toward all who sat in the darkness of ignorance, scatter also my darkness!

Righteous Father Herman, pray for us!

You, the honorable bud of the Russians, O Herman, have bloomed with the rose of the sweet love Christ, from the reek of my passions, deliver me by your prayers!

Righteous Father Herman, pray for us!

The Alaskan soil was watered by the sweat of your prayers, water also the filthy hearts of us sinners from the burning heat by springs of water.

Most Holy Theotokos, save us!

O fragrant perfume, Mary, grant purity to your hopeless and miserable servants, by the balm of your love, through the prayers of Herman the pure!

Ode 3, "The Apse of the Heavens…"

Tablet of dispassion, the boast of Valaam monastery, O pillar of watchfulness, by the rod of your God-moving prayers, O Herman, at all times strengthen, the choir of your supplicants, Father all-comely.

Righteous Father Herman, pray for us!

The impoverished natives of the Aleutian Isles have beheld a divine sight, O Herman, sleepless champion; cease not from fighting, with tears and sighs, for the pious in the midst of life's storms and troubles!

Righteous Father Herman, pray for us!

As the most ready saviour of those who turn to you, O Herman, from the enemy's wrath, keep watch always over those who joyfully sing to your labors in Alaska, for the spread of Christ's faith, O Father.

Most Holy Theotokos, save for us!

Enliven me, O Mother, who am dead by the passions, Virgin Full of Grace, with the breeze of your motherly supplications before Christ, the Divine Word of God, Whom you have ineffably born, O birthgiver of God!

Make to rise, upon those sitting in the gloom of sins, o Lightbringer Herman, the light of knowledge, peace, prudence, and love!

Turn to me, in your good favour, all praise-worthy Theotokos; look upon my grave illnesses, which painfully sting my flesh and heal the cause of my soul's pain and suffering.

Priest: Have mercy on us, O God, according to Your great love, we pray You, hear us, and have mercy.
People: Lord have mercy. (3)

Priest: Again we pray for our Archbishop (name), our Bishop (name), and all the clergy and the laity in Christ.
People: Lord have mercy. (3)

Priest: Again we pray for mercy, life, peace, health, salvation, visitation, forgiveness and remission of the sins of the servants of God, all pious and Orthodox Christians, those who reside and visit in this city, the members, council members, contributors, and benefactors of this holy church.
People: Lord have mercy. (3)

Priest: Again we pray for the servants of God ... At this time the Priest commemorates those for whom the Paraklesis is sung.
People: Lord have mercy. (3)

Priest: For You are a merciful and loving God, and to You we give glory, to the Father and the Son and the Holy Spirit, now and forever and to the ages of ages.
People: Amen.

Kathisma.
Ikos, 2nd Tone, "A fervent prayer..."
Of the Fathers of the monastery of St. Sergius, of Sarov, of Optina and Valaam, you stand as an equal, O most holy Herman, having followed the divine Apostles. Make us worthy to follow your pure paths to perfection.

Ode 4, "O Lord I have heard..."

Russia was made exalted, O divinely wise Herman, by your swaddling bands, Alaska by your labors, and we by your divine protection.

Righteous Father Herman, pray for us!

O most good gardener, Herman, by the sickle of divine grace, prune away the sinful tares of we who bless you.

Righteous Father Herman, pray for us!

Refuge of the pious, O Herman, healer and comfort of orphans, we call out to you, be the guardian of all who honor you.

Most Holy Theotokos, save for us!

Come to me, Mother of God, lead me to the path of unending bliss with Christ, your only begotten child, O Virgin.

Ode 5, "Lord Enlighten Us"

Victor over foes, Spirit-bearer Herman, give spiritual wings by piety to all who rightly magnify you.

Righteous Father Herman, pray for us!

Cut off the waves of the passions of those who flee to you, Herman, worthy Alaskan peer of the apostles, and adornment of the faith.

Righteous Father Herman, pray for us!

Bearing the Cross of Christ, O Herman, you have arrived at the rampart of the divine things within Him, plead for us who offer you praise.

Most Holy Theotokos, save us!
Perfect your Only-Begotten Son's graciousness to us, O Immaculate Virgin, who brilliantly magnify the multitude your wonders.

Ode 6, "My Petition…"

Behold, O Herman, our weakness, and by the medicine of your prayers, lighten the incurable pains of all those who sing to your sleepless labors to enlighten those who remain in the darkness of ignorance, O most divine!

Righteous Father Herman, pray for us!

The joyful making celebration in song, Divine Apostle Herman, we cry out on behalf of your day-and-night labors to acquire dispassion and perfection; show the saving path of watchfulness to those who seek your favour.

Righteous Father Herman, pray for us!

Asking, O Herman, your prayers, in order that we may beautifully scale the ascetic ladder of the virtues, O God-bearer, we praise with graceful odes the loftiness of your life and love toward all who sigh.

Most Holy Theotokos, save us!

O All-hymned Lady Theotokos, O sweetness of the light-formed angels, and delight of the chosen kind, of Herman the pure; by supplications, sweeten, by your grace, the bitterness of our sorrowful life.

Make to rise, upon those sitting in the gloom of sins, o Lightbringer Herman, the light of knowledge, peace, prudence, and love!

Turn to me, in your good favour, all praise-worthy Theotokos; look upon my grave illnesses, which painfully sting my flesh and heal the cause of my soul's pain and suffering.

Ikos in Tone 2, "Of your blood…"
Walking in the footsteps of the Apostles, unto Alaska you have brought salvation by the faith of Christ, O Herman, calling it forth from corruption, He now imploring to give each of your supplicants strength and power.

Prokeimenon
Precious in the sight of the Lord is the death of his saints **(Psalm 115:6)**
Verse: God is wonderful in His saints **(Psalm 68:36)**

Priest: Let us pray to the Lord, our God, that we may be deemed worthy to hear the Holy Gospel,
People: Lord have mercy. (3)

Priest: Wisdom, Arise, Let us hear the Holy Gospel. Peace be with all.
People: And with your spirit.

Priest: The reading of the Holy Gospel according to Luke. Let us be attentive.
People: Glory to You, O Lord, glory to You.

Priest: At that time, He came down with them and stood on a level place with a crowd of His disciples and a great multitude of people from all Judea and Jerusalem, and from the seacoast of Tyre and Sidon, who came to hear Him and be healed of their diseases, as well as those who were tormented with unclean spirits. And they were healed. And the whole multitude sought to touch Him, for power went out from Him and healed them all. Then He lifted up His eyes toward His disciples, and said: "Blessed are you poor, For yours is the kingdom of God. Blessed are you who hunger now, For you shall be filled. Blessed are you who weep now, For you shall laugh. Blessed are you when men hate you, And when they exclude you, And revile you, and cast out your name as evil, For the Son of Man's sake. Rejoice in that day and leap for joy! For indeed your reward is great in heaven, For in like manner their fathers did to the prophets.

People: Glory to You, O Lord, glory to You.

2nd Tone

Glory to the Father and the Son and the Holy Spirit.

Through the intercessions of your Righteous One, merciful One, wash away my many personal offenses.

Now and forever and to the ages of ages. Amen.

Through the intercessions of the Theotokos, merciful One, wash away my many personal offenses.

Verse: Have mercy upon me, O God, according to Your great mercy; and according to the multitude of Your compassions blot out my transgressions.

Ikos in Plagal 2nd (6th) Tone, "Having laid all their hope..."
Blessed Equal of the Apostles, the enlightener of the Aleuts, Herman widely-sung, blossom of the Russian land most-famed, through the strength of your intercessions, you stilled the all-destroying wave, and so saved your rational flock, O God bearer, restrain also the maelstrom of our love of wickedness by your grace, send your peace to us who piously keep, Father, your all-worthy memory.

Priest: O God, save Your People, and bless Your inheritance; look upon Your world with mercy and compassion; raise the Orthodox Christians to glory, and shower us with your abundant mercies, through the intercessions of our all pure Lady, the Theotokos and ever virgin Mary, through the power of the precious and life giving Cross; through the protection of the honourable, heavenly bodiless powers; of the honourable, glorious prophet, the Forerunner John the Baptist; of the holy glorious and all praised Apostles; of our holy fathers the great hierarchs and ecumenical teachers, Basil the Great, Gregory the Theologian, and John Chrysostom; Athanasios and Cyril, John the Merciful, patriarchs of Alexandria; Nicholas of Myra, Spyridon bishop of Trimythous, the wonder workers; of the holy glorious great martyrs George the triumphant, Demetrios the myrrhflowing, Theodore of Tyros and Theodore the Commander; of the holy martyrs Charalambos and Eleutherios; of the holy glorious triumphant Martyrs; of our pious and God bearing Fathers; of (the Saint of the Church); of the holy and righteous Ancestors of God, Joachim and Anna; of Saint (Name) whose memory we celebrate today; and of all Your Saints, we beseech You Lord, Who alone are all merciful; hear the prayers of us sinners and have mercy upon us.

People: Lord have mercy. (12)

Priest: By the mercy and compassion, and love of Your only begotten Son, with whom You are blessed, together with Your all holy and life giving Spirit, now and forever and to the ages of ages.
People: Amen.

Ode 7, "Coming out of Judaea..."

Having illumined the Aleut people's darkness, O Herman, by the radiance of your Orthodox words; deliver me swiftly from my reproach and affliction, and set me on the straight road to virtue.

Righteous Father Herman, pray for us!

To the prudent disciple of the Righteous Nazarios, inspired abbot of Valaam, you we hymn, Divine Herman; teach us to faithfully keep the saving commandments of the Lord.

Righteous Father Herman, pray for us!

Follower of the Philokalic ascetics and wise Paisios, O Herman, by way of your supplications, award dispassion and watchfulness upon those that now bless you with sweet-flowing songs and odes.

Most Holy Theotokos, save us!

Make us worthy, O Theotokos, to partake of the tree of life in the heavenly garden, we who have hymned you, as of the tree bearing immortal fruit for the cosmos, even the very Lord of Glory.

Ode 8, "The king of heaven…"

With sweet streams having watered the Aleutian isles, O Herman, clean my soul of filth with the hyssop of your prayers.

Righteous Father Herman, pray for us!

As a vessel of the all-capable Comforter, O Father Herman, fill the hearts of your supplicants, now filled by sorrow, with joy.

Righteous Father Herman, pray for us!

Your toils, patience in spirit and longing we honor, O Herman, with faith we seek your prayers before God.

Most Holy Theotokos, save us!

Now honoring the divine feats of Herman, we implore you, fill us, O Birth-giver of God, with the blessings of your Son.

Ode 9, "Saved through you…"

Now the people named for Christ, O Herman, faithfully keep your memory, we await your never-silent supplications before God.

Righteous Father Herman, pray for us!

Now, together with Nazarios, Seraphim of Sarov, Sergius, and the Optina Elders, we offer up praise, O Herman, as our defender.

Righteous Father Herman, pray for us!

You bless from heaven, those who sing to you now; O Herman, bless also the works of those who turn in faith to your protection.

Most Holy Theotokos, Save us!

Christ the giver of life, and your Son, send upon us, O Virgin Mother, the mercy of compassion, rich and without measure.

Megalynaria.
Truly you are worthy to be blessed, Mother of our God, the Theotokos, you the ever blessed one, and all blameless one, and the Mother of our God. * You are honored more than the Cherubim, and you have more glory, when compared, to the Seraphim; You, without corruption, did bear God, the Logos; You are the Theotokos; You do we magnify.

Rejoice, flower of the dwelling of Valaam, that in Alaska has blossomed with ascesis, O Herman, the perfume of whose pure labors and divine words wafts throughout the universe.

Rejoice, swift defender of orphans and the poor, and helper of all who groan mightily under slavery's yoke, O Herman, adornment of the Fathers.

Rejoice, Herman Divinely Bright, zealot of the Philokalia and of watchfulness; hail, renunciatory, simple, pure, humble-minded, and selfless prayer.

Watch over and sanctify, O Herman, the Aleutian people, with the choir of the pious throughout the world, through your care and the power of the Most-Holy Cross, O Equal-to-the-Apostles.

You have been revealed, O Child of Russia, as a gentle lover of Christ from youth to maturity, and his Gospel you proclaimed, O Herman; having been shown a divine inheritance in Alaska.

Still the waves of the passions, by your fervent supplications before the Most High, O Herman, as by your prayers you stopped the wave with the shaking of the sea, O angelic Father.

(The Megalynarion of the church is chanted)

With the hosts of Angels, God's messengers, with the Lord's Forerunner, and Apostles, the chosen twelve, with the saints most holy, and with you, the Theotokos, we seek your intercession for our salvation.

Trisagion
Holy God, Holy Mighty, Holy Immortal, have mercy upon us (3).

Glory to the Father and the Son and the Holy Spirit, now and forever and to the ages of ages. Amen.

Most holy Trinity, have mercy upon us; Lord, pardon our sins; Master, forgive our transgressions; Holy One, visit and heal our infirmities, for Your name's sake.
Lord have mercy (3).

Glory to the Father, and the Son and the Holy Spirit, now and forever and to the ages of ages. Amen.

Our Father, Who is in heaven, hallowed be Your name. Your kingdom come, Your will be done, on earth as it is in heaven. Give us this day our daily bread; and forgive us our trespasses as we forgive those who trespass against us. And lead us not into temptation but deliver us from evil.

Priest: For Yours is the kingdom and the power and the glory, of the Father and the Son and the Holy Spirit, now and forever and to the ages of ages.
People: Amen.

Troparion, in Plagal 1st (5th) Tone "The co-eternal word..."

Rising as a star of prayer and watchfulness in the dwelling of Valaam, unto the natives of Alaska you have spread the light of the Gospel, O Herman, following the steps of the Apostles in these last times, O blessed; and now by your prayers to the Lord, scatter the darkness of our passions.

Glory to the Father and the Son and the Holy Spirit. Both now...

Hail, gateway impassible of the Lord, rejoice, * the wall and shelter of those who take refuge in your arms * stormless paradise, rejoice, O Maid who knew not man * and yet ineffably did birth * the Creator and our God, * therefore cease not interceding * for those who sing you your praises * and worship Him the Lord God Whom you bore.

Priest: Have mercy on us, O God, according to your great love, we pray to you, hear us, and have mercy.
People: Lord, have mercy. (3)

Priest: Again we pray for our Archbishop (name), and our Bishop (name), and all the clergy and the laity in Christ.
People: Lord have mercy. (3)

Priest: Again we pray for mercy, life, peace, health, salvation, visitation, forgiveness, and remission of the sins of the servants of God, all pious and Orthodox Christians, those who reside and visit in this city, the members, council members, contributors, and benefactors of this holy church.
People: Lord have mercy. (3)

Priest: Again we pray for the servants of God ... At this time the Priest commemorates those for whom the Paraklesis is sung.
People: Lord have mercy. (3)

Priest: Again we pray for the safekeeping of this holy church and this city, and of all cities and towns from pestilence, famine, earthquake, flood, fire and the sword, from invasion of enemies, civil war, and unforeseen death; for His mercy, that He

will be kind to entreat as our good God, Who loves all people and that He may turn away and scatter all wrath and disease that moves against us, and deliver us from His impending, justified chastisement, and have mercy on us.
People: Lord have mercy. (3)

Priest: Again we pray that the Lord God will hear the voices of the petitions of us sinners and have mercy on us.
People: Lord have mercy. (3)

Priest: Hear us, O God, our Saviour, the hope of all the ends of the earth, and of those who are far off upon the sea; and show compassion on us, O Master, on our many sins, and have mercy upon us.
People: Lord, have mercy. (3)

Priest: For you are a merciful and loving God, and to You we give glory, to the Father and the Son and the Holy Spirit, now and forever and to the ages of the ages.
People: Amen.

Priest: Glory to You, O God, our hope, glory to You. May Christ our true God, through the intercessions of Your all pure and blameless holy Mother; of the holy glorious and praise worthy Apostles; of the holy glorious and triumphant martyrs; of (the Saint of the Church); of the holy righteous ancestors of God Joachim and Anna; of Saint (name) whose memory we celebrate today; and of all the Saints, have mercy and save us, as a good and loving God.

Ikos in the 2nd Tone, "As from the Cross..."

Free from the waves of the passions and the whirlpool of errors, O God-seer Herman, the one who fervently flees to your aid, and cries out in faith, "O Divine Apostle, fame of Alaska, the one who saved the Aleutian isles from the tidal wave, speed from heaven to help those that honor you!"

O Lady, present the entreaties of your slaves, and release us from all necessity and affliction.

All my hope I place in you, Mother of God, protect me under your shelter.

Priest: Through the prayers of our Holy Fathers, Lord Jesus Christ, our God, have mercy and save us.
People: Amen.

Akathist

Kontakion 1

O Chosen Doer of Wonders, most glorious favorite of Christ, our God bearing Father Herman, Alaska's adornment, the joy of all Orthodox in America. We sing to you, our heavenly protector and powerful intercessor before God, these songs of praise. Cease not to pray for your children, who cry fervently to you:

Rejoice our blessed Father Herman of Alaska, America's most glorious doer of wonders.

Ikos 1

The Creator of the Angelic Hosts, called you, Father Herman, to proclaim the Orthodox faith in the new land and to be the founder of the monastic way in the remote lands of the North. You were sent, as was the Apostle Paul, to those sitting in darkness so that the light of Orthodoxy might brightly shine to all the ends of the world. We, the inhabitants of the American continents, bring you this thanksgiving and sing this song of praise to you, our heavenly protector:

Rejoice, our Father Herman, our glory, our adornment;
Rejoice, bringer of the light of the true faith to our lands;
Rejoice, gatherer of your own glory by your great spiritual effort;
Rejoice, most honored branch of Valaam Monastery;
Rejoice, praise and joy of the Church in America;
Rejoice, comforter and protector of all of us;
Rejoice, our blessed Father Herman of Alaska, America's most glorious doer of wonders.

Kontakion 2

In your early youth, O Blessed One, enkindled by the flame of love for the Lord, you desired to serve God and Him alone. As an offering, you dedicated your youth to God, beginning your journey from the hermitage of Valaam, where many novices sang ceaselessly to God: Alleluia!

Ikos 2

The Most High granted you spiritual wisdom in your youth that you might know the beauty and sweetness of heaven. For this reason, the wise Igumen Nazary, teacher of the blessed Seraphim of Sarov, taught you God's wisdom and the Lord's way. Therefore, the Holy Church praises you:

Rejoice, glorious Herman dedicator of your youth to Christ;
Rejoice, disciple together with Seraphim of Sarov;
Rejoice, performer of spiritual labors in glorious Valaam;
Rejoice, honored by all the brethren of Valaam Monastery;
Rejoice, learner of spiritual wisdom in Valaam;
Rejoice, glorified now by the Orthodox Church;
Rejoice, our blessed Father Herman of Alaska, America's most glorious doer of wonders.

Kontakion 3
The power of the Most High directed the divinely-wise primate of the Church in Russia, Gabriel, to send preachers of the Orthodox Faith to Alaska. The apostolic choice fell on you, O Blessed Herman, therefore, all the people enlightened by the Light of Christ through your labors and the personal example of your life, sang to the Lord: Alleluia!

Ikos 3
Showing great zeal not only in your spiritual labors as a novice, but also in your Apostolic fervor as you preached to a people sitting in darkness, you, O Blessed Herman, revealed the light of Christ to them with great power. Remembering your labors as a novice and your efforts to preach; with love we praise you:

Rejoice, uncomplaining giver of obedience to your Igumen;
Rejoice, beginner of a long journey to preach;
Rejoice, steadfast in your love for the land of your birth;
Rejoice, inflamed with love for your new found home;
Rejoice, initiator of the monastic way in America;
Rejoice, zealous preacher of the Orthodox Faith;
Rejoice, our blessed Father Herman of Alaska, America's most glorious doer of wonders.

Kontakion 4
O Blessed Father Herman, you endured storms of evil attacks and sorrows, by your efforts you persevered in this new land. Therefore, Christ glorified you with the gift of foresight, enriching you with miracles, granting you the Kingdom of Heaven where, together with the angels, you praise God in song: Alleluia!

Ikos 4
Hearing of the miracles revealed to your people when a forest fire and tidal wave were made to cease by your prayers, we implore you from the depths of our hearts and entreat you to aid us who call to you:

Rejoice, ascetic and prophet glorified by God;
Rejoice, holy favorite of God;
Rejoice, our intercessor and healer;
Rejoice, helper of many who called out to you;
Rejoice, healer of many afflicted and suffering;
Rejoice, our merciful and humble Father;
Rejoice, our blessed Father Herman of Alaska, America's most glorious doer of wonders.

Kontakion 5
O Blessed One, you have shone like the North Star on Spruce Island, the New Valaam, illuminating all of America with the brightness of your love and prayer, full of God's power, so that from every corner of it the Orthodox people will sing fervently to God: Alleluia!

Ikos 5

Observing your humility, all are in awe of you, O Father Herman, for your rigorous asceticism and perseverance in monastic struggles. In this you followed the example of Anthony of the Caves, the founder of monasticism in Russia, even as he that of Anthony the Great, first monk of the world. You, the founder of monasticism in our land, chose in your great humility the way of a simple monk. Therefore, the holy choir of hierarchs and hieromonks sings these songs of praise to you:

Rejoice, founder of monasticism in our land;
Rejoice, imitator of Anthony the Great and Anthony of the Caves;
Rejoice, crowned, as they were, with heavenly glory;
Rejoice, promising the building of a glorious hermitage where you labored;
Rejoice, giver of your relics to your hermitage;
Rejoice, revealing a source of miracles from them to all the world;
Rejoice, our Blessed Father Herman of Alaska, America's most glorious doer of wonders.

Kontakion 6

The wilderness of the North proclaims your works and miracles, revealing you to be a new branch of the vineyard of the Church of Russia in America. The forests and wilderness are permeated with your prayers. Following the example of the ancient hermits, you cried out in the silence of the night to God: Alleluia!

Ikos 6

You enlightened the people who were living in darkness; you showed them an example of the monastic way of life. O our Godbearing Father Herman, pray that we all, giving thanks to the Lord, may ceaselessly sing you these words of praise:

Rejoice, first saint of our land;
Rejoice, founder of the monastic way in our land;
Rejoice, faithful servant of the Holy Trinity;
Rejoice, humble founder of the church of the Resurrection;
Rejoice, glorious hermit of the hermitage of Spruce Island;
Rejoice, loving father of the children who came to him;
Rejoice, our blessed Father Herman of Alaska, America's most glorious doer of wonders.

Kontakion 7

The Lord chose you, O Blessed One, to bring the light of the knowledge of God to the land of the Aleuts and there to sow the seeds of the Orthodox faith. You taught all to embrace the true faith and to call out to God: Alleluia.

Ikos 7

You reached the heights through prayer, O Blessed One. You did not forget those who were in the depths of the earth. You manifested great concern for homeless orphans, building an orphanage and a school for them. You taught them the commandments of the Lord. Therefore, because of these labors, accept from us these praises:

Rejoice, defender of the poor and orphaned;
Rejoice, their good protector;
Rejoice, builder of a home for the orphaned;
Rejoice, servant to God with your labors;
Rejoice, provider of earthly bread to the orphaned;
Rejoice, nourisher of orphans with words of eternal life;
Rejoice, our blessed Father Herman of Alaska, America's most glorious doer of wonders.

Kontakion 8

The Lord who loves mankind, O Blessed One, gave you the gifts of foresight and healing in His desire to manifest through you a source of compassion for his people. You brought them to the love of God through your works and many words of instruction. Enlightened by the light of your spiritual labors, the people called to the Lord: Alleluia!

Ikos 8

The people newly illumined by the light of the Christian Faith came to you in times of illness and sorrow. As a father who loved his children, you interceded for all, bringing forth healing and comfort to all who came to you for help. Your glory has gone forth throughout all Alaska and we, your spiritual children, glorify you:

Rejoice, our merciful father;
Rejoice, our unmercenary and gracious physician;
Rejoice, merciful healer of our infirmities;
Rejoice, our speedy helper in time of trouble and need;
Rejoice, foreseer of coming events as of the present;
Rejoice, perceptive reprover of hidden transgressions;
Rejoice, our blessed Father Herman of Alaska, America's most glorious doer of wonders.

Kontakion 9

O Blessed One, you spoke with angels, according to your own testimony, relating how the angels came to you in your hermitage and you had sweet conversation with them. Now you are in the Kingdom of Heaven where with hosts of angels you pray ceaselessly to the Creator of all and the Maker of this praise: Alleluia!

Ikos 9

Who can enumerate the miracles witnessed by your people? The waves of the sea and a fire in the forest were calmed by your prayers. When there was a great tidal wave, you caused the stormy seas to cease by your prayers before the icon of the Mother of God, saying: "The water shall not go beyond this line." Therefore, we sing to you thus:

Rejoice, wondrous pacifier of the waters;

Rejoice, most glorious savior from a forest fire;
Rejoice, savior of the hierarch Innocent who called to you from the sea;
Rejoice, because of his prayer to you the wind at sea changed;
Rejoice, revealer of many miracles during your life;
Rejoice, revealer of many miracles even after your death;
Rejoice, our Blessed Father Herman of Alaska, America's most glorious doer of wonders.

Kontakion 10

We bring to you a song of praise, O blessed father, concerning your righteous life. We sing praises of your honored death. You foreknew the day and hour of your blessed end. Most glorious also was your burial. For forty days a great storm raged at sea and your prophecy concerning your burial was fulfilled. Your disciple Gerasim, sensing a wondrous fragrance at the time of your death, sang to God: Alleluia!

Ikos 10

You were a most glorious doer of wonders during your life, O Father. At your death you manifested this wondrous miracle: your body remained incorrupt in the chapel for many days after your death. The Aleut people who saw a flaming pillar ascending to Heaven at the hour of your death, sang to you thus:

Rejoice, for your righteous end has assured us of your holiness;
Rejoice, for your ascension to Heaven was like a pillar of fire;
Rejoice, for your relics exuding an odor of sanctity are left as our inheritance;
Rejoice, for many miracles are made manifest at your reliquary;
Rejoice, giver to us of a source of holy water and healing;
Rejoice, for from this water many who are afflicted received healing;
Rejoice, our blessed Father Herman of Alaska, America's most glorious doer of wonders.

Kontakion 11

O Holy Father, from your hermitage in the North, in the midst of the wilds of nature, you sang ceaseless praises to the Holy Trinity. Moved by the Spirit you foresaw the great flowering of this vineyard planted in the soil of America and you called out with the angels of Heaven: Alleluia!

Ikos 11

To all future members of the monastic order, you are a source of light and illumination. For you foretold, O Blessed One, the founding of a monastery and of an archbishop's throne in this land. Today a choir of hierarchs and of monastics glorifies you in these words:

Rejoice, instructor of monastics and converser with angels;
Rejoice, most glorious founder of the ascetic way in our land;
Rejoice, foreseer of the growth of this great vineyard of Christ;
Rejoice, fulfillment of this prophecy to the coming generations;
Rejoice, giver of a true image of the monastic way;

Rejoice, for your love is made manifest to all;
Rejoice, our blessed Father Herman of Alaska, America's most glorious doer of wonders.

Kontakion 12
Seeing your grace and your great boldness before God, we entreat you, O blessed father Herman, to pray fervently to the Lord, that He will protect His Holy Church from faithlessness and schism, from false teaching and willfulness, that we may sing to God Who has dealt bountifully with us: Alleluia!

Ikos 12
We praise your glorification, O Blessed One, we bless you, O most powerful Intercessor and Protector of our Church, and with love we sing to you:

Rejoice, protector of all who honor you;
Rejoice, speedy responder and helper to all;
Rejoice, founder of Orthodoxy in our land;
Rejoice, strengthener of those who come to the Orthodox Faith;
Rejoice, most glorious protector of the Church in America;
Rejoice, her first saint and her wondrous Father;
Rejoice, our blessed Father Herman of Alaska, America's most glorious doer of wonders.

Kontakion 13
O Most glorious favorite of God, Our Blessed Father Herman, Accept this humble prayer we offer up in praise to you. Standing now before the Throne of the Almighty Lord, ceaselessly pray for us. In joy we sing to God:

Alleluia! Alleluia! Alleluia!

(Repeat Kontakion Thirteen 3 times)
(Then continue below)

Ikos 1
The Creator of the Angelic Hosts, called you, Father Herman, to proclaim the Orthodox faith in the new land and to be the founder of the monastic way in the remote lands of the North. You were sent, as was the Apostle Paul, to those sitting in darkness so that the light of Orthodoxy might brightly shine to all the ends of the world. We, the inhabitants of the American continents, bring you this thanksgiving and sing this song of praise to you, our heavenly protector:

Rejoice, our Father Herman, our glory, our adornment;
Rejoice, bringer of the light of the true faith to our lands;
Rejoice, gatherer of your own glory by your great spiritual effort;
Rejoice, most honored branch of Valaam Monastery;
Rejoice, praise and joy of the Church in America;
Rejoice, comforter and protector of all of us;

Rejoice, our blessed Father Herman of Alaska, America's most glorious doer of wonders.

Kontakion 1
O Chosen Doer of Wonders, most glorious favorite of Christ, our God bearing Father Herman, Alaska's adornment, the joy of all Orthodox in America. We sing to you, our heavenly protector and powerful intercessor before God, these songs of praise. Cease not to pray for your children, who cry fervently to you:

Rejoice our blessed Father Herman of Alaska, America's most glorious doer of wonders.

Prayer to St. Herman of Alaska
O most wondrous, favorite of God, our blessed Father Herman, as a good laborer you did your great spiritual work in a harsh climate in this land. In your service to God, you were faithful in the little things. And, as the Lord said: "You have been faithful over a little, I well set you over much." Now, when this word has been fulfilled in you, the Lord has set you over our whole Church, as her heavenly protector. We all call to you in fervent prayer: Entreat the Lord to keep our Holy Church steadfast in Orthodoxy and to reveal her to be an adornment of our land.

May He protect her from all the dark powers of the enemy and drive out all adversaries. May He grant us purity of faith and beauty of soul. Pray He will grant us all the spirit of peace and love, the spirit of humility and meekness and drive out the sin of pride. Save us from self praise.

Be our guard from false teachings. Give healing to the sick; to the sorrowful be a comfort. To those who hunger for spiritual truth, give the heavenly food; that we may attain our true desire, and receive the good reward at the final Judgment. With all the saints we will praise with song: the Life creating Trinity, the Ineffable Father, the True and Only-Begotten Son, the Comforter, Holy Spirit, forever.

Amen.

Biography

Commemorated on August 9

A spiritual mission was organized in 1793, made up of monks of the Valaam Monastery. They were sent to preach the Word of God to the native inhabitants of northwestern America, who only ten years before had come under the sovereignty of Russia. Saint Herman was among the members of this Mission.

Saint Herman came from a family of merchants of Serpukhov, a city of the Moscow Diocese. His name before he was tonsured, and his family name are not known. (The monastic name is given when a monk takes his vows). He had a great zeal for piety from youth, and at sixteen he entered monastic life. (This was in 1772, if we assume that Herman was born in 1756, although sometimes 1760 is given as the date of his birth.) First he entered the Trinity-Sergius Hermitage which was located near the Gulf of Finland on the Peterhof Road, about 15 versts (about 10 miles) from Saint Petersburg.

Miraculous Healing

At the Saint Sergius Hermitage there occurred the following incident to Father Herman. On the right side of his throat under his chin there appeared an abscess. The swelling grew rapidly, disfiguring his face. It became difficult for him to swallow, and the odor was unbearable. In this critical condition Father Herman awaited death. He did not appeal to a physician of this world, but locking his cell he fell before an icon of the Mother of God. With fervent tears he prayed, asking of Her that he might be healed. He prayed the whole night. Then he took a wet towel and with it wiped the face of the Most Holy Mother, and with this towel he covered the swelling. He continued to pray with tears until he fell asleep from sheer exhaustion on the floor. In a dream he saw the Virgin Mary healing him.

When Herman awoke in the morning, he found to his great surprise that he was fully healed. The swelling had disappeared, even though the abscess had not broken through, leaving behind but a small mark as though a reminder of the miracle. Physicians to whom this healing was described did not believe it, arguing that it was necessary for the abscess to have either broken through of its own accord or to have been cut open. But the words of the physicians were the words of human experience, for where the grace of God operates there the order of nature is overcome. Such occurrences humble human reason under the strong hand of God's Mercy.

Life at Valaam

For five or six years Father Herman continued to live in the Saint Sergius Hermitage, and then he transferred to the Valaam Monastery, which was widely scattered on the large islands in the waters of the great Lake Ladoga. He came to love the Valaam haven with all his soul, as he came to love its unforgettable Superior, the pious Elder Nazarius, and all the brethren. He wrote to Father

Nazarius later from America, "Your fatherly goodness to me, humble one, will be erased out of my heart neither by the terrible, unpassable Siberian lands, nor by the dark forests. Nor will it be wiped out by the swift flow of the great rivers; nor will the awful ocean quench these feelings. In my mind I imagine my beloved Valaam, looking to it beyond the great ocean." He praised the Elder Nazarius in his letters as, "the most reverend, and my beloved father," and the brethren of Valaam he called, "my beloved and dearest." The place where he lived in America, deserted Spruce Island, he called "New Valaam." And as we can see, he always remained in spiritual contact with his spiritual homeland, for as late as 1823, that is after thirty years of his life within the borders of America, he wrote letters to the successor of Father Nazarius, the Igumen Innocent.

Father Barlaam, later Igumen of Valaam, and a contemporary of Father Herman, who accepted his tonsure from Father Nazarius, wrote thus of the life of Father Herman.

"Father Herman went through the various obediences here, and being 'well disposed toward every thing' was in the course of events sent to Serdobol to oversee there the work of quarrying marble. The Brothers loved Father Herman, and awaited impatiently his return to the cloisters from Serdobol. Recognizing the zeal of the young hermit the wise elder, Father Nazarius, released him to take abode in the wilderness. This wilderness was in the deep forest about a mile from the cloister: to this day this place has retained the name 'Herman's.' On holy days, Father Herman returned to the monastery from the wilderness. Then it was that at Little Vespers he would stand in the choir and sing in his pleasant tenor the responses with the brethren from the Canon, 'O Sweetest Jesus, save us sinners. Most Holy Theotokos, Save us,' and tears would fall like hail from his eyes."

The First Mission to America

In the second half of the 18th century the borders of Holy Russia expanded to the north. In those years Russian merchants discovered the Aleutian Islands which formed in the Pacific Ocean a chain from the eastern shores of Kamchatka to the western shores of North America. With the opening of these islands there was revealed the sacred necessity to illumine with the light of the Gospel the native inhabitants. With the blessing of the Holy Synod, Metropolitan Gabriel gave to the Elder Nazarius the task of selecting capable persons from the brethren of Valaam for this holy endeavor. Ten men were selected, and among them was Father Herman. The chosen men left Valaam for the place of their great appointment in 1793. (The members of this historical mission were: Archimandrite Joseph (Bolotoff); the hieromonks Juvenal, Macarius, Athanasius, Stephan, and Nectarius; hierodeacons Nectarius and Stephen; and the monks Joasaph and Herman.)

As a result of the holy zeal of the preachers the light of the evangelic sermon quickly poured out among the sons of Russia, and several thousand pagans accepted Christianity. A school for the education of newly-baptized children was organized, and a church was built at the place where the missionaries lived. But by the inscrutable providence of God the general progress of the mission was unsatisfactory. After five years of very productive labor, Archimandrite Joasaph, who had just been elevated to the rank of bishop, was drowned with his party. (This occurred on the Pacific Ocean between Kamchatka and the Aleutian Islands. The ship, Phoenix, one of the first sea-going ships built in Alaska, sailed from Okhotsk carrying the first Bishop for the American Mission and his party. The Phoenix was caught in one of the many storms which periodically sweep the northern Pacific, and the ship and all hands perished together with Bishop Joasaph and his party.) Before this the zealous Hieromonk Juvenal was granted the martyr's crown. The others died one after another until in the end only Father Herman remained. The Lord permitted him to labor longer than any of his brethren in the apostolic task of enlightening the Aleutians.

The New Valaam — Spruce Island

In America, Father Herman chose as his place of habitation Spruce Island, which he called New Valaam. This island is separated by a strait about a mile and a quarter wide from Kodiak Island on which had been built a wooden monastery for the residence of the members of the mission, and a wooden church dedicated to the Resurrection of the Savior. (New Valaam was named for Valaam on Lake Ladoga, the monastery from which Father Herman came to America. It is interesting to note that Valaam is also located on an island, although, this island is in a fresh water lake, whereas, Spruce Island is on the Pacific Ocean, although near other islands and the Alaskan mainland.)

Spruce Island is not large, and is almost completely covered by a forest. Almost through its middle a small brook flows to the sea. Herman selected this picturesque island for the location of his hermitage. He dug a cave out of the ground with his own hands, and in it he lived his first full summer. For winter there was built for him a cell near the cave, in which he lived until his death. The cave was converted by him into a place for his burial. A wooden chapel, and a wooden house to be used as a schoolhouse and a guest house were built not too distant from his cell. A garden was laid out in front of his cell. For more than forty years Father Herman lived here.

Father Herman's Way of Life

Father Herman himself spaded the garden, planted potatoes and cabbage and various vegetables in it. For winter, he preserved mushrooms, salting or drying them. The salt was obtained by him from ocean water. It is said that a wicker basket in which the Elder carried seaweed from the shore, was so large that it was difficult for one person to carry. The seaweed was used for fertilizing the soil. But to the astonishment of all, Father Herman carried a basket filled with seaweed for a long distance without any help at all. By chance his disciple, Gerasim, saw him one winter night carrying a large log which normally would be carried by four men; and he was bare footed. Thus worked the Elder, and everything that he acquired as a result of his immeasurable labors was used for the feeding and clothing of orphans and also for books for his students.

His clothes were the same for winter as for summer. He did not wear a shirt; instead he wore a smock of deer skin, which he did not take off for several years at a time, nor did he change it, so that the fur in it was completely worn away, and the leather became glossy. Then there were his boots or shoes, cassock (podrasnik), an ancient and faded out cassock (riasa) full of patchwork, and his headdress (klobuk). He went everywhere in these clothes, and at all times; in the rain, in snowstorms, and during the coldest freezing weather. In this, Father Herman followed the example of many Eastern Ascetic Fathers and Monks who showed the greatest concern for the welfare and needs of others. Yet, they themselves wore the oldest possible clothes to show their great humility before God, and their detachment from worldly things.

A small bench covered with a time-worn deerskin served as Father Herman's bed. He used two bricks for a pillow; these were hidden from visitors by a skin or a shirt. There was no blanket. Instead, he covered himself with a wooden board which lay on the stove. This board Father Herman himself called his blanket, and he willed that it be used to cover his remains; it was as long as he was tall. "During my stay in the cell of Father Herman," writes the creole Constantine Larionov, "I, a sinner, sat on his 'blanket'-and I consider this the acme of my fortune!" ('creole' is the name by which the Russians referred to the children of mixed marriages of native Indians of Alaska, Eskimo and Aleuts with Russians.)

On the occasions when Father Herman was the guest of administrators of the American Company and in the course of their soul-saving talks he sat up with them until midnight. He never spent the night with them, but regardless of the weather he always returned to his hermitage. If for some extraordinary reason it was necessary for him to spend the night away from his cell, then in the morning the bed which had been prepared for him would be found untouched; the Elder not having slept at all. The same was true in his hermitage where having spent the night in talks, he never rested.

The Elder ate very little. As a guest, he scarcely tasted the food, and remained without dinner. In his cell his dinner consisted of a very small portion of a small fish or some vegetables. His body, emaciated as a result of his labors, his vigils, and fasting, was crushed by chains which weighed about sixteen pounds. These chains are kept to this day in the chapel. Telling of these deeds of Father Herman, his disciple, the Aleut Ignaty Aligyaga, added, "Yes, Apa led a very hard life, and no one can imitate his life!" (The Aleutian word "Apa" means Elder or grandfather, and it is a name indicative of the great affection in which he was held).

Our writing of the incidents in the life of the Elder deal, so to speak, with the external aspects of his labor. "His most important works," says the Bishop Peter, "were his exercises in spiritual endeavor in his isolated cell where no one saw him, but outside the cell they heard him singing and celebrating services to God according to the monastic rule." This witness of the Bishop is supported by the following answers of Father Herman, himself: "How do you manage to live alone in the forest, Father Herman? Don't you ever become lonesome?" He answered, "No I am not there alone! God is here, as God is everywhere. The Holy Angels are there.

With whom is it better to talk, with people, or with Angels? Most certainly with Angels."

Father Herman and the Native Alaskans

The way in which Father Herman looked upon the natives of America, how he understood his own relations with them, and how he was concerned for their needs he expressed himself in one of his letters to the former administrator of the colony, Simeon Yanovsky. He wrote, "Our Creator granted to our beloved homeland this land which like a newly-born babe does not yet have the strength for knowledge or understanding. It requires not only protection, because of its infantile weakness and impotence, but also his sustenance. Even for this it does not yet have the ability to make an appeal on its own behalf. And since the welfare of this nation by the Providence of God, it is not known for how long, is dependent on and has been entrusted into the hands of the Russian government which has now been given into your own power, therefore I, the most humble servant of these people, and their nurse (nyanka) stand before you in their behalf, write this petition with tears of blood. Be our Father and our Protector. Certainly we do not know how to be eloquent, so with an inarticulate infant's tongue we say: Wipe away the tears of the defenseless orphans, cool the hearts melting away in the fire of sorrow. Help us to know what consolation means."

The Elder acted the way he felt. He always interceded before the governors on behalf of those who had transgressed. He defended those who had been offended. He helped those who were in need with whatever means he had available. The Aleuts, men, women and children, often visited him. Some asked for advice, others complained of oppression, others sought out defense, and still others desired help. Each one received the greatest possible satisfaction from the Elder. He discussed their mutual difficulties, and he tried to settle these peacefully. He was especially concerned about reestablishing understanding in families. If he did not succeed in reconciling a husband and wife, the Elder prevailed upon them to separate temporarily. The need for such a procedure he explained thus, "it is better to let them live apart, or believe me, it can be terrible if they are not separated. There have been incidents when a husband killed his wife, or when a wife destroyed her husband."

Father Herman especially loved children. He made large quantities of biscuits for them, and he baked cookies (krendelki) for them; and the children were fond of the Elder. Father Herman's love for the Aleuts reached the point of self-denial.

An Epidemic Strikes

A ship from the United States brought to Sitka Island, and from there to Kodiak Island, a contagious disease, a fatal illness. It began with a fever, a heavy cold, and difficult respiration, and it ended with chills; in three days the victim died. On the island there was neither a doctor nor medicine. The illness spread rapidly through the village, and then throughout the nearby areas. The disease affected all, even infants. The fatalities were so great that for three days there was no one to dig graves, and the bodies remained unburied. An eyewitness said, "I cannot imagine anything more tragic and horrible than the sight which struck me when I visited an Aleutian 'Kazhim'. This was a large building, or barracks, with dividing sections, in which the Aleuts lived with their families; it contained about 100 people. Here some had died, their cold bodies lay near the living; others were dying; there were groans and weeping which tore at one's soul."

"I saw mothers over whose bodies cold in death crawled a hungry child, crying and searching in vain for its food...My heart was bursting with compassion! It seemed that if anyone could paint with a worthy brush the full horror of this tragic scene, that he would have successfully aroused fear of death in the most embittered heart." Father Herman, during this terrible sickness which lasted a whole month, gradually dying out towards the end, visited the sick, never tiring. He admonished them in their fear, prayed, brought them to penance, or prepared them for death. He never spared himself.

Father Herman as a Spiritual Teacher

The Elder was concerned in particular for the moral growth of the Aleuts. With this end in mind a school was built for children-the orphans of the Aleuts. He himself taught them the Law of God and church music. For this same purpose he gathered the Aleuts on Sunday and Holy Days for prayer in the chapel near his cell. Here his disciple read the Hours and the various prayers while the Elder himself read the Epistle and Gospel. He also preached to them. His students sang, and they sang very well. The Aleuts loved to hear his sermons, gathering around him in large numbers. The Elder's talks were captivating, and his listeners were moved by their wonderous power. He himself writes of one example of the beneficial results of his words.

"Glory to the holy destinies of the Merciful God! He has shown me now through his unfathomable Providence a new occurrence which I, who have lived here for twenty years had never seen before on Kodiak," he wrote. "Recently after Easter, a young girl about twenty years of age who knows Russian well, came to me. Having heard of the Incarnation of the Son of God and of Eternal Life, she became so inflamed with love for Jesus Christ that she does not wish to leave me. She pleaded eloquently with me. Contrary to my personal inclination and love for solitude, and despite all the hindrances and difficulties which I put forward before accepting her, she has now been living near the school for a month and is not lonesome. I, looking on this with great wonder, remembered the words of the Savior: 'that which is hidden from the wise and learned is revealed to babes'" (Matthew 11:25).

This woman lived at the school until the death of the Elder. She watched for the good conduct of the children who studied in his school. Father Herman willed that after his death she was to continue to live on Spruce Island. Her name was Sophia Vlasova.

Yanovsky writes about the character and the eloquence of the talks of the Elder thus: "When I met Father Herman I was thirty years old. I must say that I was educated in the naval corps school; that I knew many sciences having read extensively. But to my regret, the Science of sciences, that is the Law of God, I barely remembered the externals—and these only theoretically, not applying them to life. I was a Christian in name only, but in my soul and in reality, I was a freethinker. Furthermore, I did not admit the divinity and holiness of our religion, for I had read through many atheistic works. Father Herman recognized this immediately and he desired to reconvert me. To my great surprise he spoke so convincingly, wisely—and he argued with such conviction—that it seemed to me that no learning or worldly wisdom could stand one's ground before his words. We conversed with him daily until midnight, and even later, of God's love, of eternity, of the salvation of souls, and of Christian living. From his lips flowed a ceaseless stream of sweet words! By these continual talks and by the prayers of the holy Elder the Lord returned me completely to the way of Truth, and I became a real Christian. I am indebted for all this to Father Herman; he is my true benefactor.

"Several years ago," continues Yanovsky, "Father Herman converted a certain naval captain G. to Orthodoxy from the Lutheran Faith. This captain was well educated. Besides many sciences, he was well versed in languages. He knew Russian, English, German, French, Italian and also some Spanish. But for all this he could not resist the convictions and proofs of Father Herman. He changed his faith and was united to the Orthodox Church through Chrismation. When he was leaving America, the Elder said to him while they were parting, "Be on guard, if the Lord should take your wife from you then do not marry a German woman under any circumstance. If you do marry a German woman, undoubtedly she will damage your Orthodoxy." The Captain gave his word, but he failed to keep it. The warning of the Elder was prophetic. Indeed, after several years the Captain's wife did die, and he married a German woman. There is no doubt that his faith weakened or that he left it; for he died suddenly without penance."

Further on Yanovsky writes, "Once the Elder was invited aboard a frigate which came from Saint Petersburg. The Captain of the frigate was a highly educated man, who had been sent to America by order of the Emperor to make an inspection of all the colonies. There were more than twenty-five officers with the Captain, and they also were educated men. In the company of this group sat a monk of a hermitage, small in stature and wearing very old clothes. All these educated conversationalists were placed in such a position by his wise talks that they did not know how to answer him. The Captain himself used to say, 'We were lost for an answer before him.'

"Father Herman gave them all one general question: 'Gentlemen, What do you love above all, and what will each of you wish for your happiness?' Various answers were offered ... Some desired wealth, others glory, some a beautiful wife, and still others a beautiful ship he would captain; and so forth in the same vein. 'Is it not true,' Father Herman said to them concerning this, 'that all your various wishes can bring us to one conclusion—that each of you desires that which in his own understanding he considers the best, and which is most worthy of his love?' They all answered, 'Yes, that is so!' He then continued, 'Would you not say, Is not that which is best, above all, and surpassing all, and that which by preference is most worthy of love, the Very Lord, our Jesus Christ, who created us, adorned us with such ideals, gave life to all, sustains everything, nurtures and loves all, who is Himself Love and most beautiful of all men? Should we not then love God above every thing, desire Him more than anything, and search Him out?'

"All said, 'Why, yes! That's self-evident!' Then the Elder asked, 'But do you love God?' They all answered, 'Certainly, we love God. How can we not love God?' 'And I a sinner have been trying for more than forty years to love God, I cannot say that I love Him completely,' Father Herman protested to them. He then began to demonstrate to them the way in which we should love God. 'If we love someone,' he said, 'we always remember them; we try to please them. Day and night our heart is concerned with the subject. Is that the way you gentlemen love God? Do you turn to Him often? Do you always remember Him? Do you always pray to Him and fulfill His holy commandments?' They had to admit that they had not! 'For our own good, and for our own fortune,' concluded the Elder, 'let us at least promise ourselves that from this very minute we will try to love God more than anything and to fulfill His Holy Will!' Without any doubt this conversation was imprinted in the hearts of the listeners for the rest of their lives.'

"In general, Father Herman liked to talk of eternity, of salvation of the future life, of our destinies under God. He often talked on the lives of the Saints, on the Prologue, but he never spoke about anything frivolous. It was so pleasant to hear him that those who conversed with him, the Aleuts and their wives, were so captivated by his talks that often they did not leave him until dawn, and then they left him with reluctance;" thus witnesses the Creole, Constantine Larionov.

A Description of Father Herman

Yanovsky writes a detailed description of Father Herman. "I have a vivid memory," he said, "Of all the features of the Elder's face reflecting goodness; his pleasant smile, his meek and attractive mien, his humble and quiet behavior, and his gracious word. He was short of stature. His face was pale and covered with wrinkles. His eyes were greyish-blue, full of sparkle, and on his head there were a few gray hairs. His voice was not powerful, but it was very pleasant." Yanovsky relates two incidents from his conversations with the Elder. "Once," he writes, "I read to Father Herman the ode, 'God,' by Derzhavin. The Elder was surprised, and entranced. He asked me to read it again. I read it once more, "Is it possible that a simple, educated man wrote this?" he asked. "Yes, a learned poet," I answered. "This has been written under God's inspiration," said the Elder.

The Martyrdom of Peter

"On another occasion I was relating to him how the Spanish in California had imprisoned fourteen Aleuts, and how the Jesuits were forcing all of them to accept the Catholic Faith. But this Aleut would not agree under any circumstances, saying, 'We are Christians.' The Jesuits protested, 'That's not true; you are heretics and schismatics. If you do not agree to accept our faith then we will torture all of you.' Then the Aleuts were placed in cells until evening; two to a cell. At night the Jesuits came to the prison with lanterns and lighted candles. They began to persuade the

Aleuts in the cell once again to accept the Catholic Faith. 'We are Christians,' was the answer of the Aleuts, 'and we will not change our Faith.' Then the Jesuits began to torture them, at first the one while his companion was the witness. They cut the toes off his feet, first one joint and then the other joint. And then they cut the first joint on the fingers of the hands, and then the other joint. Afterwards they cut off his feet, and his hands; the blood flowed. The martyr endured all and steadfastly insisted on one thing: 'I am a Christian.' In such suffering, he bled to death. The Jesuit promised to torture to death his comrades also on the next day.... But that night an order was received from Monterey stating that the imprisoned Aleuts were to be released immediately, and sent there under escort. Therefore, in the morning all were dispatched to Monterey with the exception of the martyred Aleut. This was related to me by a witness, the same Aleut who was the comrade of the tortured Aleut. Afterwards he escaped from imprisonment, and I reported this incident to the supreme authorities in Saint Petersburg. When I finished my story, Father Herman asked, 'And how did they call the martyred Aleut?' I answered, 'Peter; I do not remember his family name.' The Elder stood up before an icon reverently, made the sign of the Cross and pronounced, 'Holy newly-martyred Peter, pray to God for us!'"

The Spirit of Father Herman's Teaching

In order to express the spirit of Father Herman's teaching, we present here a quotation from a letter that was written by his own hand.

"The empty years of these desires separate us from our heavenly homeland, and our Love for these desires and our habits clothe us, as it were, in an odious dress; it is called by the Apostle 'the external (earthy) man' (1 Corinthians 15:47). We who are wanderers in the journey of this life call to God for aid. We must divest ourselves of this repulsiveness, and put on new desires, and a new love for the coming age. Thus, through this we will know either an attraction or a repulsion for the heavenly homeland. It is possible to do this quickly, but we must follow the example of the sick, who wishing for desired health, do not stop searching for means of curing themselves. But I am not speaking clearly."

Not desiring anything for himself in life, when he first came to America, he refused in his humility the dignity of hieromonk and archimandrite, deciding to remain forever a common monk, Father Herman, without the least fear before the powerful, strove with all sincerity for God. With gentle love, and disregarding the person, he criticized many for intemperate living, for unworthy behavior, and for oppressing the Aleuts. Evil armed itself against him and gave him all sorts of trouble and sorrow. But God protected the Elder. The Administrator of the Colony, Yanovsky, not having yet seen Father Herman, after receiving one of those complaints, had already written to Saint Petersburg of the necessity of his removal. He explained that it seemed that he was arousing the Aleuts against the administration. But this accusation turned out to be unjust, and in the end Yanovsky was numbered among the admirers of Father Herman.

Once an inspector came to Spruce Island with the Administrator of the Colony and with company employees to search through Father Herman's cell. This party expected to find property of great value in Father Herman's cell. But when they found nothing of value, an employee of the American Company, Ponomarkhov, began to tear up the floor with an axe, undoubtedly with the consent of his seniors. Then Father Herman said to him, "My friend, you have lifted the axe in vain; this weapon shall deprive you of your life." Some time later people were needed at Fort Nicholas, and for that reason several Russian employees were sent there from Kodiak; among them was Ponomarkhov; there the natives of Kenai cut off his head while he slept.

The Temptations of Father Herman

Many great sorrows were borne by Father Herman from evil spirits. He himself revealed this to his disciple, Gerasim. Once when he entered Father Herman's cell without the usual prayer he received no answer from Father Herman to any of his questions. The next day Gerasim asked him the reason for his silence. On that occasion Father Herman said to him, "When I came to this island and settled in this hermitage the evil spirits approached me ostensibly to be helpful. They came in the form of a man, and in the form of animals. I suffered much from them; from various afflictions and temptations. And that is why I do not speak now to anyone who enters into my presence without prayer." (It is customary among devout laymen, as well as clergy, to say out loud a prayer, and upon hearing a response ending with Amen, to enter and go to the icon in the room to reverence it, and to say a prayer before greeting the host).

Supernatural Gifts from God

Herman dedicated himself fully for the Lord's service; he strove with zeal solely for the glorification of His Most Holy Name. Far from his homeland in the midst of a variety of afflictions and privations Father Herman spent several decades performing the noblest deeds of self-sacrifice. He was privileged to receive many supernatural gifts from God.

In the midst of Spruce Island down the hill flows a little stream into the sea. The mouth of this stream was always swept by surf. In the spring when the brook fish appeared the Elder raked away some of the sand at its mouth so that the fish could enter, and at their first appearance they rushed up the stream. His disciple, Ignaty, said, "it was so that if 'Apa' would tell me, I would go and get fish in the stream!" Father Herman fed the birds with dried fish, and they would gather in great numbers around his cell. Underneath his cell there lived an ermine. This little animal can not be approached when it has had its young, but the Elder fed it from his own hand. "Was not this a miracle that we had seen?" said his disciple, Ignaty. They also saw Father Herman feeding bears. But when Father Herman died the birds and animals left; even the garden would not give any sort of crops even though someone had willingly taken care of it, Ignaty insisted.

On Spruce Island there once occurred a flood. The inhabitants came to the Elder in great fear. Father Herman then took an icon of the Mother of God from the home where his students lived, and placed it on a "laida" (a sandy bank) and began to pray. After his prayer he turned to those present and said,"Have no fear, the water will not go any higher than the place where this holy icon stands." The words of the Elder were fulfilled. After this he promised the same aid from this holy icon in the future, through the intercessions of the Mother of God. He entrusted the icon to his disciple Sophia; in case of future floods the icon was to be placed on the "laida." This icon is preserved on the island to this day.

At the request of the Elder, Baron F. P. Wrangel wrote a letter to a Metropolitan (his name is not known) which was dictated by Father Herman. When the letter was completed and read, the Elder congratulated the Baron upon his attaining the rank of admiral. The Baron was taken aback. This was news to him. It was confirmed, but only after an elapse of some time, and just before he departed for Saint Petersburg.

Father Herman said to the administrator Kashevarov, from whom he accepted his son from the font (during the Sacrament of Baptism), "I am sorry for you, my dear 'kum.' It's a shame; the change will be unpleasant for you." In two years, during a change of administration, Kashevarov was sent to Sitka in chains.

Once, the forest on Spruce Island caught fire. The Elder, with his disciple Ignaty, in a thicket of the forest made a belt about a yard wide in which they turned over the moss. They extended it to the foot of the hill. The Elder said, "Rest assured, the fire will not pass this line." On the next day, according to the testimony of Ignaty, there was no hope of salvation (from the fire) and the fire, pushed by a strong wind, reached the place where the moss had been turned over by the Elder. The fire ran over the moss and halted, leaving untouched the thick forest which was beyond the line.

The Elder often said that there would be a Bishop for America; this at a time when no one even thought of it, and there was no hope that there would be a Bishop for America. This was related by Bishop Peter, and his prophecy was fulfilled in time.

"After my death," said Father Herman, "there will be an epidemic, many people shall die during it, and the Russians shall unite the Aleuts." And so it happened. It seems that about a half a year after his passing, there was a smallpox epidemic; the death rate in America during the epidemic was tremendous. In some villages, only a few inhabitants remained alive. This led the administration of the colony to unite the Aleuts; the twelve settlements were consolidated into seven.

"Although a long time shall elapse after my death, I will not be forgotten" said Father Herman to his disciples. "My place of habitation will not remain empty. A monk like me, who will be escaping from the glory of men, will come and he will live on Spruce Island, and Spruce Island will not be without people." (This prophecy has now been fulfilled in its entirety. Just such a monk as Father Herman described lived on Spruce Island for many years; his name was Archimandrite Gerasim, who died on October 13, 1969. This monk took on himself the responsibility of taking care of the Chapel under which the Elder Herman was first buried. Metropolitan Leonty, soon after his elevation to the primacy of the Russian Orthodox Church in America, made a pilgrimage to Spruce Island, and the grave of Saint Herman.)

Prophecies for the Future

The Creole Constantine, when he was not more than twelve years old, was asked by Father Herman, "My beloved one, what do you think; this chapel which they are building now, will it ever stand empty?" The youngster answered, "I do not know, Apa." "Indeed," said Constantine, "I did not understand his question at that time, even though the whole conversation with the Elder remains vivid in my memory." The Elder remained silent for some time, and then said, "My child, remember, in time there will be a monastery in this place."

Father Herman said to his disciple the Aleut Ignaty Aligyaga, "Thirty years shall pass after my death, and all those living on Spruce Island will have died, but you alone will remain alive. You will be old and poor when I will be remembered." And indeed after the death of Father Herman thirty years passed when they were reminded of him, and they began to gather information and facts about him, on the basis of which his Life was written. "It is amazing," exclaims Ignaty, "how a man like us could know all this so long before it happened! However, no, he was no ordinary man! He knew our thoughts, and involuntarily he led us to the point where we revealed them to him, and we received counsel from him."

"When I die," the Elder said to his disciple, "you will bury me alongside Father Joasaph. You will bury me by yourself, for you will not wait for the priest. Do not wash my body. Lay it on a board. Clasp my hands over my chest, wrap me in my mantia (the monk's outer cloak), and with its wings cover my face and place the klobuk (monastic head covering) on my head. If anyone wishes to bid farewell to me, let them kiss the Cross. Do not show my face to anyone...."

The Repose of Father Herman

The time of the Elder's passing had come. One day he ordered his disciple Gerasim to light a candle before the Icons, and to read the Acts of the Holy Apostles. After some time his face glowed brightly and he said in a loud voice, "Glory to Thee, O Lord!" He then ordered the reading to be halted, and he announced that the Lord had willed that his life would now be spared for another week. A week later, again by his orders, candles were lit, and the Acts of the Holy Apostles were read. Quietly, the Elder bowed his head on Gerasim's chest; the cell was filled with a sweet-smelling odor; and his face glowed, and Father Herman was no more! Thus he died in blessedness, he passed away in the sleep of a righteous man in the eighty-first year of his life of great labor the 25th day of December 1837. (It was the 13th of December according to the Julian Calendar, although there are some records which state that he died on November 28th and was buried on December 26th).

Those sent with the sad news to the harbor returned to announce that the administrator of the colony Kashevarov had forbidden the burial of the Elder until his own arrival. He also ordered that a finer coffin be made for Father Herman, and that he would come as soon as possible and would bring a priest with him. But then a great wind came up, a rain fell, and a terrible storm broke. The distance from the harbor to Spruce Island is not great—about a two hour journey—but no one would agree to go to sea in such weather. Thus it continued for a full month, and although the body lay in state for a full month in the warm house of his students, his face did not undergo any change at all, and not the slightest odor emanated from his body. Finally, through the efforts of Kuzma Uchilischev, a coffin was obtained. No one arrived from the harbor, and the inhabitants of Spruce Island alone buried the remains of the Elder in the ground. Thus the words which Father Herman uttered before his death were fulfilled. After this the wind quieted down, and the surface of the sea became as smooth as a mirror.

One evening, above the village Katani (on Afognak) an unusual pillar of light which reached up to heaven was seen above Spruce Island. Astonished by the miraculous appearance, experienced elders and the Creole Gerasim Vologdin and his wife Anna said, "It seems that Father Herman has left us," and they began to pray. After a time, they were informed that the Elder had indeed passed away that very night. This same pillar was seen in various places by others. On the night of his death a vision was seen in another of the settlements on Afognak; it seemed as though a man was rising from Spruce Island into the clouds.

The disciples buried their father, and placed a wooden memorial marker above his grave. Father Peter Kashevarov, the priest on Kodiak, says, "I saw it myself, and I can say that today it seems as though it had never been touched by time; as though it had been cut this day."

Having witnessed the life of Father Herman glorified by his zealous labors, having seen his miracles, and the fulfillment of his predictions, finally having observed his blessed falling asleep, "in general, all the local inhabitants," Bishop Peter witnesses, "have the highest esteem for him, as though he was a holy ascetic, and they are fully convinced that he has found favor in the presence of God."

In 1842, five years after the passing away of the Elder, Archbishop Innocent of Kamchatka and the Aleutians, was near Kodiak on a sailing vessel which was in great distress. He looked to Spruce Island, and said to himself, "If you have found favor in God's presence, Father Herman, then may the wind change." It seems as though not more than fifteen minutes had passed, said the bishop, when the wind became favorable, and he successfully reached the shore. In thanksgiving for being saved, Archbishop Innocent himself conducted a Memorial Service (Panikhida) over the grave of the blessed Father Herman.

O Holy Father Herman of Alaska, pray unto God for us!